Surviving Myself:
If You Knew My Story, You Would Understand My Praise

Copyright © 2023

All rights reserved.

The author reserves all rights to be recognized as the owner of this work. You may not sell or reproduce any part of this book without written consent from the copyright owner.

First paperback edition December 2023

Book design by Angela Staples Robertson

ISBN: 9798871295601

Imprint: Independently published by Angela Staples Robertson

This autobiography is dedicated to my grandmother, Ma, whose unwavering love and wisdom continue to guide me even in her absence. Your legacy lives on through me, and I dedicate this book to the woman whose strength and grace inspired my journey of self-preservation and praise.

- Angela

Table of Contents

Table of Contents	5
Prologue: The Uncharted Path	7
Chapter 1: Roots of Resilience: Early Childhood and Family Dynamics	11
Chapter 2: The Guiding Light: Ma's Unwavering Support	23
Chapter 3: Teenage Chapter Motherhood: A Hidden Journey	28
Chapter 4: A Second Mother: The Complex Legacy of My Grandmother	34
Chapter 5: The Power of Education: Pursuing Academic Success	39
Chapter 6: Breaking Stereotypes: Career and Professional Achievements	52
Chapter 7: Balancing Act: Juggling Motherhood and Career	62
Chapter 8: Building a Support System: Friendships and Relationships	79
Chapter 9: Trials and Triumphs: Overcoming Adversity	88
Chapter 10: Lessons for the Next Generation: Parenting and Mentorship	102
Epilogue: Looking Back and Moving Forward	107
Conclusion: Acknowledgments and Gratitude	112

Prologue: The Uncharted Path

In the tapestry of life, each thread weaves a unique story—a story sculpted by the hands of destiny and the choices we make in the intricate fabric of existence. My journey is a testament to this profound truth—a path less traveled, a narrative forged from the fires of resilience, the hammer of determination, and the unwavering spirit that can rise from the ashes of adversity.

As I sit down to etch these words onto the canvas of my life story, I am reminded of the countless moments that have propelled me to this juncture—the moments that have shaped the woman I am today. My tale begins with twists and turns—ones that many might deem insurmountable. At the tender age of three, I found myself entrusted to the care of my grandmother, a guardian angel in her own right. Then, as a teenager, barely old enough to grasp the complexities of the world, I was thrust into the daunting role of motherhood. The world was quick to label me, to consign me to the statistics of circumstance. But what they couldn't see was the fire that burned within me—a fire stoked by the love of God and the strength instilled in me by my grandmother and other guardian angels placed on this earth.

Within the pages of this book, I will gently unfurl the layers of my life, one chapter at a time. From the tempestuous years of my youth to the soaring triumphs that followed, this narrative is a testament to the power of unwavering resolve, the profound beauty of unanticipated support, and the indomitable bonds that can crystallize amidst the most improbable circumstances.

My earnest hope is that, by sharing my testament to the grace of God, I may ignite a spark within others who confront similar trials. May they find the belief in their own potential, summon the strength to surmount adversity, and dare to dream beyond the stifling confines of their circumstances. Life's journey seldom follows a linear and easy path, but it is in the bends, twists, and unforeseen diversions that we unearth our true selves—the bedrock of resilience and our capacity for extraordinary feats. Remember, dear reader, that God resides not only in the destination but in the very journey itself.

So, with an open heart and a willing spirit, accompany me on this voyage of retrospection and revelation. Together, let us explore the zeniths and nadirs, the trials and conquests, and the unwavering love and support that have molded the person I have become. This is my story—a chronicle of hope, tenacity, and the uncharted path that guided me to a place of accomplishment and fulfillment.

"I CAN DO ALL THIS THROUGH HIM WHO GIVES ME STRENGTH"

Philippians 4:13

(NIV)

Chapter 1: Roots of Resilience: Early Childhood and Family Dynamics

The story of my early childhood is a tapestry woven with threads of both hardship and love, with the central figures being my grandmother, Kathryn, whom I affectionately called Ma, and my birth mother, Des—a complex, elusive presence that ebbed in and out of my life like the tide.

A Childhood Shrouded in Uncertainty

My earliest memories are marked by a small, modest house tucked away in a quiet neighborhood in south Memphis, its walls bearing witness to a tumultuous family history. It was within those walls that I celebrated birthdays, received nightly tickles and hugs, and felt the first pangs of confusion and abandonment.

My mother, a young woman trapped in her own tumultuous life, struggled to provide the stability and care I needed. Her own battle with an abusive relationship and a lifestyle fraught with drugs and recklessness created an environment that was far from nurturing for a child.
I remember one day we were in an apartment, and her boyfriend started yelling at her about something. The next thing I remember is both of us on the floor; she happened to be holding me in her arms. I had to be around 3 years old. I guess traumatic events do etch themselves in your memory regardless of age. It wasn't long before my grandmother 'helped' my mother make the agonizing decision to leave me with her, a decision that would forever alter the course of my life.

Kathryn, my Ma, emerged as a dominant force of strength and love in my life. She was a young grandmother, shouldering the responsibilities of motherhood once more, and she did it with grace and tenacity that left an indelible mark on my heart.
Ma worked tirelessly, often taking on multiple odd jobs to make ends meet. Our modest home was a testament to her unwavering dedication to provide for me and create a sense of stability amidst the chaos that had initially defined my early years. We lived in a small 2-bedroom,

1-bath home on Gage Street. To a curious 3-year-old like me, our home felt like a mansion. It was a place of wonder, where every corner held the promise of adventure.

It's So Pink

As I walked across the cold hardwood floor of my childhood bedroom, the sea of pink enveloped me like a warm, comforting hug. It was as if the walls themselves whispered tales of fairy tales and adventures waiting to unfold. Pink adorned every corner of the room, from the delicate curtains that fluttered in the breeze to the soft, plush bedding that cradled me at night. Pink was more than just a color to me as a little girl; it was a symbol of enchantment, imagination, and all the beautiful possibilities that childhood held. In my eyes, pink represented a world of wonder, where dreams came to life and where I could be anything I wanted to be.

Pink, with its soft and gentle hues, was a color that embodied the innocence and purity of childhood. It was the shade of cotton candy at the fair, the delicate petals of an azalea bush in spring, and the rosy cheeks of a beloved baby doll. To me, pink represented the magic of make-believe, where ordinary objects transformed into extraordinary treasures, and every day held the potential for extraordinary adventures.

In that enchanted castle of a bedroom, pink was a canvas for my imagination to run wild. It was the color of the make-believe princess gowns I'd twirl in, pretending to attend grand balls and rescue kingdoms. It was the shade of the tea set I'd use to host royal tea parties for my stuffed animal friends, complete with imaginary conversations and make-believe treats.

But pink was more than just a color—it was a feeling. It was the warmth of my grandmother's embrace when she tucked me in at night, the scent of freshly baked pies wafting from the kitchen, and the sound of bedtime stories that transported me to far-off lands. It was the comfort of being loved and cherished, wrapped in the soft, rosy embrace of my safe haven.

As I grew older, the enchantment of pink may have faded, but the memories of my pink sanctuary remained etched in my heart. It was a reminder of the magic of childhood, the boundless possibilities of dreams, and the unwavering love and care that surrounded me. Pink, in all its shades and hues, would forever hold a special place in my heart—a symbol of the innocence, wonder, and beauty of those precious early years.

The pink walls were adorned with beautiful paintings and mirrors that covered an entire wall, reflecting the joy and wonder that radiated from my little self.

Two twin-size beds with white, frilly bedspreads sat side by side, beckoning me to countless adventures and sweet dreams. My great grandmother, a master seamstress, had hand-sewn those bedspreads with love, using white fabric adorned with intricate lace trim. Matching pillowcases completed the ensemble, and as I nestled into those beds, I felt the warmth of generations of family love enveloping me.

In every corner of the room, my own little world took shape. A dresser, chest of drawers, and desk with a bookshelf hutch were my treasures, each piece telling a story of my grandmother's dedication to making my childhood special. The dresser held my carefully folded clothes, the chest hid away my most treasured toys, and the desk was a world of creativity and exploration. The bookshelf hutch was a treasure trove of adventures waiting to be discovered. Books of all shapes and sizes beckoned from the shelves, their spines bearing the promise of countless journeys to distant lands and imaginary realms. Ma understood the power of knowledge and imagination, and she nurtured my love for books from a young age.

A Gift of Generations: Love and Family Heritage

In my room, I not only had a physical sanctuary but also a symbolic one—a testament to the love and dedication of generations that came before me. The hand-sewn bedspread, crafted by my great grandmother's loving hands, was a tangible connection to my family's history. It was a reminder that love and creativity were woven into the very fabric of our family.

As a 3-year-old, I couldn't fully grasp the significance of the space I called my own. Still, I could feel the love that permeated every inch of my dream bedroom. It was a place where I could be a princess, a ballerina, or a storyteller, all within the comfort of my four pink walls.

Education was a cornerstone of Ma's values. Despite her own struggle with formal education, she was a firm believer in its power to transcend circumstances. She instilled in me a thirst for knowledge, teaching me to read and write before I even entered school. It was through her encouragement and love of learning that I developed a passion for education that would shape my future.

While Ma was the steady and loving presence in my life, my birth mother's presence remained a fleeting and unpredictable force. She would drift in and out of my life like a phantom, appearing when it suited her and disappearing when it did not. Each return brought a glimmer of hope, a yearning for a mother's love, but it was always followed by the harsh reality of her lifestyle choices.

Her life was a stark contrast to the stability Ma

provided. She was entangled in an abusive relationship, and her choices often led her down a dark path of drug use and an iniquitous lifestyle. My young mind struggled to comprehend the tumultuous world she inhabited, and I learned to brace myself for her inevitable departures.

There was one particular day that shone like a brilliant star in the night sky—the day I came home from school to find my mother, a rare and cherished presence in my life, hiding in one of my twin beds. It was a moment of pure, unadulterated joy that would forever be etched in my heart.

I remember that day vividly. The sun streamed through the pink curtains in my room, casting a warm glow on the delicate lace trim of my bedspread. As I entered the room, a peculiar sight greeted me—a lump beneath the covers of one of the twin beds.
My heart leaped with excitement and curiosity as I approached the bed. I gingerly pulled back the bedspread, and to my utter astonishment, there she was—my mother. Her eyes sparkled with love and delight as she revealed herself, and in that moment, time stood still. "Surprise!," she yelled, her voice loud with excitement. I couldn't contain my happiness; my mother was home, and I was the happiest child on earth.

Those days following were nothing short of magical. We shared meals, laughter danced in the air, and the room filled with the sound of our playful banter. It was days of simple pleasures—a mother and her child reunited, reveling in the ordinary moments that most take for granted.

We played games, talked about school, and I regaled her with stories of my adventures. In those fleeting hours, my mother was not just a visitor; she was a part of our daily life, and it felt like the world had finally fallen into place.

But as the week drew to a close, reality set in. It was time for me to return home from school, and I eagerly anticipated another joyful reunion. However, when I entered my room, there was no lump beneath the bedspread, no warm presence waiting to surprise me. My mother was nowhere to be found.

In my desperation, I pulled back the bedspread, hoping against hope that she might be hiding once again, playing an elaborate game of hide-and-seek. But the bed was empty, and the truth hit me like a tidal wave—I was alone once more.

Devastation washed over me, and I couldn't hold back the tears. The joy I had felt just days earlier had turned into heartache. The unpredictability of my mother's presence in my life had once again left an indelible mark on my young heart.

The rollercoaster of emotions that came with my mother's sporadic presence and absence may have been unbearable if it were not for God keeping me covered. These moments of joy and heartache would shape my understanding of love, resilience, and the enduring bond between a mother and her child.

Daddy's Home

I always considered myself to be a daddy's girl. My dad lived just two blocks away from my grandmother's house, and he was an unforgettable presence in my early life. Although he wasn't present at my birth, as he was in Atlanta attending a school for fashion to learn the art of tailoring clothes, he rushed back home as soon as he heard of my arrival. His commitment to being a father to his baby girl was unwavering, and it marked the beginning of a cherished relationship.

Every weekend, I eagerly made my way to my dad's house. It was a place of joy and camaraderie, where he was known as the life of the party, and everyone in the neighborhood seemed to be drawn to his magnetic personality. The sizzling sounds of something delicious on his grill became a weekend ritual, and the air was always filled with laughter and the chatter of friends and neighbors.

One of the most vivid memories I hold close to my heart is spending Christmas at my dad's house for the first time. I had my own special place there – a waterbed that I would sleep in alone, and I loved it. But this Christmas was different; it was my first away from my grandmother's home. As I lay there, I couldn't help but wonder how Santa would find me in this new place. Would he know I was at my dad's house this year?

In my childlike innocence, I decided to go to bed extra early on Christmas Eve, hoping that it would somehow assist Santa in his mission. The anticipation and excitement kept me awake for a while, but eventually, I drifted into slumber.

When I woke up on that magical Christmas morning and rubbed the sleep from my eyes, I couldn't believe what I saw. The room was filled with the soft, warm glow of the morning sun, and there, surrounding me, were all the toys I had ever wished for, wrapped in colorful paper and adorned with ribbons and bows. It was a sight that took my breath away.

This Christmas was etched in my memory, not just for the gifts, but for the warmth and love that permeated my dad's home. It was a time when I realized that the greatest gift of all was the presence of family, the love and connection that bound us together.

My dad's love, his infectious spirit, and his commitment to being there for me, especially during those early years, became the foundation upon which I built my own resilience. He showed me that even in the face of challenges and adversity, love and family could provide a solid and unwavering support system. It was a lesson that would shape my outlook on life and become a source of strength as I navigated the challenges that lay ahead.

During those formative years of my life, when the absence of my mother's consistent presence left a void that was often difficult to bear, my grandmother, Ma, emerged as the unwavering beacon of support and love that guided me through the labyrinth of childhood. Alongside her, my dad played a pivotal role, being a constant source of love and care that provided me with the strength to navigate life's challenges.

"Can a mother forget the baby at her breast and have no compassion on the child she has borne? Though she may forget, I will not forget you!"

ISAIAH 49:15 (NIV)

Chapter 2: The Guiding Light: Ma's Unwavering Support

During those formative years of my life, when the absence of my mother's consistent presence left a void that was often difficult to bear, my grandmother, Ma, emerged as the constant beacon of support and love that guided me through the labyrinth of childhood.

Seeing the Spark: Ma's Belief in My Potential

Ma saw something in me that others might have overlooked—I was smart. It was her keen insight and belief in my potential that laid the foundation for my journey toward education and self-discovery. At the tender age of four, with Ma's patient guidance, I took my first steps into the world of reading. She was my first teacher, my constant companion in the realm of books.

As the years passed, Ma recognized the importance of fostering my intellect. She enrolled me in early learning centers, nurturing my thirst for knowledge and creativity. But it was during these early years that I began to see the evidence of God's grace at work in my life.

I often marveled at how God's grace had placed Ma in my life. She was not just my grandmother; she was a divine instrument, a guiding force chosen by a higher power. Her unwavering belief in my potential, her dedication to my education—all of these were manifestations of God's grace, providing me with the tools I needed to navigate a challenging path.

Ma was relentless in her pursuit of providing me with the best educational opportunities. She scoured the city to find the finest schools that could nurture my potential. It was during those early years of schooling that my true academic prowess began to shine.

By the time I reached fourth grade, my reading equivalency was akin to that of an eleventh grader—an achievement that was a testament to Ma's unwavering dedication to my education. She believed in me when I struggled to believe in myself, and she pushed me to excel academically, instilling in me the belief that knowledge was the key to a brighter future.

God's grace was evident in the opportunities that came my way. It was as though doors of opportunity swung open effortlessly, guiding me toward a path of academic excellence. Ma's tenacity and the divine intervention of God's grace were intertwined, propelling me forward in my educational journey.

While Ma recognized the importance of fostering my intellectual growth, she also understood the value of a well-rounded childhood. She knew that dwelling on the absence of my mother could be emotionally taxing, so she kept me involved in a myriad of activities.

I played soccer and joined the cheer team, learning the value of teamwork and discipline, and I became a Girl Scout, where I forged friendships and learned important life skills. These activities not only kept me focused but also provided a sense of belonging and purpose during times when questions about my mother's absence weighed heavily on my young heart.

As I look back on those formative years, I see God's grace in the moments of joy and camaraderie that I experienced in those activities. The friendships I formed and the life skills I acquired were invaluable, shaping me into the resilient individual I was becoming.

The Lingering Pain: Unanswered Questions

Despite Ma's best efforts, the pain of my mother's absence still lingered. I couldn't help but wonder what was so wrong with me that my own mother didn't want to be a part of my life. It was a question that gnawed at my self-esteem and fueled my determination to prove my worth, not just to others but to myself.

Isaiah 49:15 (NIV)
"Can a mother forget the baby at her breast and have no compassion on the child she has borne? Though she may forget, I will not forget you!"

In the chapters that follow, you will witness the impact of Ma's unwavering support on my life, intertwined with the undeniable presence of God's grace. Together, they would shape the young woman I was becoming, reminding me that even in the face of adversity, God's grace and love were ever-present, guiding me through the challenges of life. Ma was not just my grandmother; she was a vessel of God's grace, lighting my path toward success and self-discovery.

2 CORINTHIANS 4:8-9 (NIV)

"We are hard pressed on every side, but not crushed; perplexed, but not in despair; persecuted, but not abandoned; struck down, but not destroyed."

Chapter 3: Teenage Chapter Motherhood: A Hidden Journey

My journey into motherhood was a secret I held close to my heart, a hidden chapter in my life that unfolded with all the complexities and challenges that come with being a teenage mother.

A Love Story: The Beginning of It All

It all began with falling head over heels in love with a boy—a boy who was two grades ahead of me, a football player, and someone I, a cheerleader, couldn't resist. We were inseparable, and our love was a whirlwind that swept us off our feet.
But as our love deepened, so did the realization that we had made choices that would change the course of our lives forever. I knew I was pregnant, a secret I guarded fiercely. Fear gripped me, not just fear of the impending

responsibilities but also fear of disappointing my family, who had placed high hopes on my future.

As the weeks passed, I grappled with the physical changes that came with pregnancy. People around me began to notice, and I struggled to maintain the facade of "just gaining weight." It was a lonely and isolating experience, pretending to be unaffected by the profound transformation taking place within me.

One day, my grandmother, the perceptive and loving figure in my life, looked at me with a knowing gaze and said the words I had been dreading: "You are pregnant." I denied it vehemently, clinging to the illusion that I could keep my secret hidden. But she knew me better than anyone else, and she wasn't about to let me face this journey alone.

My grandmother took action, determined to provide me with the support and guidance I needed. She had my aunt administer a pregnancy test, and the result was undeniable—it was positive. The truth hung heavily in the air, and there was no more room for denial.

Desperate to find a solution, my grandmother took me to clinics, hoping for an alternative to the path we were reluctantly treading. But at each clinic, we received the same heartbreaking verdict—I was too far along to terminate the pregnancy. The weight of our situation was inescapable, and the reality of impending motherhood loomed large.

My grandmother, a strong advocate for family and stability, took a brave step by revealing my pregnancy to the boy's family. Their initial excitement was short-lived, as my grandmother disclosed our intention to give the baby up for adoption. It was a decision that carried both pain and hope, a choice made with the best interests of the child in mind.

Solitude and Isolation: Summer of 1995

The summer of 1995 was unlike any other, a time when solitude and isolation became the dominant themes of my life as I grappled with the life-altering decision to place my baby up for adoption. The support—or lack thereof—from my family and community during this period would leave an indelible mark on my heart. I carried a burden of guilt for not being strong enough to speak up.

After the painful decision to pursue adoption, my grandmother, the guiding force in my life, believed it was best to keep this chapter of our lives hidden from the rest of the family and the community. It was a choice made out of love and concern, an attempt to shield me from judgment and preserve a sense of normalcy. I knew her purpose but it left scars and trauma for my adolescent self to try and unpack.

I was hidden away for two long months, separated from my parents, my relatives, and the familiar faces of my community. It was a lonely summer, one where I missed out on family trips, cherished holidays like Memorial Day and the Fourth of July, and the comforting presence of loved ones. It felt as though I was being punished, and I questioned why God had chosen this path for me.

God works in mysterious ways, often using people on this Earth to shape our destinies. Someone had left a message on my dad's phone, a message that revealed my secret—a message that I had had a baby. My stepmother, sensing the urgency of the situation, called me and allowed me to hear the message firsthand. She asked me if it was true, and without hesitation, I confirmed that it was.

In that pivotal moment, my father rushed to my side, a whirlwind of emotions and determination. He asked me a question that would change everything: Did I want to raise my son? My answer was a resounding yes.

With my father's unwavering support, I embarked on a new journey—one of motherhood and family unity. We moved in with my father, my stepmother, and my siblings, creating a loving and stable environment for Michael to grow and thrive. It was a fresh start, a chance for redemption and a future that was brighter than I had ever dared to imagine.

This period of solitude and isolation shaped my perspective on life, love, and the importance of support from those around us. It was a summer that tested my resilience, my faith, and my belief in the possibility of finding strength in the most unexpected places. It gave me witness to the transformative power of love, the resilience of the human spirit, and the profound impact of family support. The bond between a mother and her child, once tested by the adoption process, would now become an unbreakable force, guiding us through the challenges and joys of life's ever-unfolding journey.

"For the Lord gives wisdom; from his mouth comes knowledge and understanding."

PROVERBS 2:6 (NIV)

Chapter 4: A Second Mother: The Complex Legacy of My Grandmother

My grandmother, Ma, was a formidable presence in my life, a second mother who left an indelible mark on my upbringing. While her influence was undeniable, it was a complex and multifaceted relationship filled with lessons, challenges, and a deep well of love.

Matter of Fact and Expectations of Perfection

Ma was a woman of unwavering conviction, and her approach to life was characterized by a matter-of-fact demeanor. She had high expectations, often expecting nothing less than perfection from those she loved. Her standards were exacting, a reflection of her desire to see her family succeed in a world that had not always been kind to her.

Her pursuit of excellence was not rooted in cruelty but rather in her belief that we were capable of achieving greatness. She saw potential in all of us, and she pushed us to reach beyond our perceived limits. Although her insistence on perfection could be daunting, it instilled in me the importance of setting high standards and striving for excellence.

Ma's love was not expressed in conventional ways. She was not emotionally expressive, a trait born from the childhood traumas she had endured. Crying was discouraged, and emotions were often kept in check. However, as a child, she did show me her love through hugs, kisses, and unwavering support.

Her independence and dedication to her work as a civil servant were further testament to her resilience and determination. Ma had survived domestic abuse and had her own dreams and ambitions. She longed to be loved and to succeed in the eyes of her own mother, seeing as Ma had also been a teenage mother.

Ma's love language was one of action. She would wake up early in the morning to prepare breakfast, ensure that my clothes were neatly pressed, and attend every school event, no matter how small. Her actions spoke volumes, even if her words did not. She taught me that love could be demonstrated through deeds, through sacrifice, and through unwavering support.

Ma's critique of appearance, behavior, and perception was a constant presence in my life. She had a sharp eye for detail and an unyielding demand for excellence. Her expectations, while challenging, pushed me to strive for the best in all that I did. However, her critical nature could also be overwhelming, leading to moments of self-doubt and insecurity.

It took me years to realize that her critiques were not meant to belittle me but to help me grow. She wanted me to be strong, resilient, and capable of facing the world's challenges head-on. Her unrelenting standards were her way of preparing me for the harsh realities of life.

As I reflect on my own life, I see how much I have become like her—a testament to the profound influence she had on me. My love for her remains unchanged, and I carry her lessons with me as I navigate the complexities of my own journey.

Proverbs 2:6 (NIV)
"For the Lord gives wisdom; from his mouth comes knowledge and understanding."

In the chapters that follow, you will delve deeper into the impact of Ma's presence in my life. Her legacy, both the challenges and the love, would continue to shape the person I was becoming. Ma's influence, a reflection of her own survival and resilience, would serve as a guiding force in my pursuit of a better future for myself and my son, Michael. Through the wisdom gained from her lessons, I would find strength to overcome adversity and strive for excellence in all that lay ahead.

"Trust in the Lord with all your heart and lean not on your own understanding; in all your ways submit to him, and he will make your paths straight."

Proverbs 3: 5 - 6 (NIV)

Chapter 5: The Power of Education: Pursuing Academic Success

My pursuit of academic success was a journey marked by significant changes, challenges, and the unwavering determination to overcome obstacles for the sake of my dreams and my son,Michael.

A Change in Course: Leaving Private School

I was told I would not amount to anything by keeping my baby. I had to prove everyone wrong. The decision to raise Michael had altered the trajectory of my life. I had to leave my beloved private school, a place where I had thrived academically. The financial burden of my education in that environment was no longer sustainable. Instead, my stepmother enrolled me in one of the top public schools in the city. It was a shift that brought both opportunities and challenges.

My stepmother recognized my intelligence and provided invaluable support in my academic journey. She played a crucial role in caring for Michael on her days off, allowing me to attend school and pursue my education. My other grandmother also stepped in to help with childcare, creating a support network that was essential to my success.

Romans 12:10 (NIV)
"Be devoted to one another in love. Honor one another above yourselves."

Despite the challenges, I was determined to continue excelling academically. I was enrolled in all Honors classes as I entered the 11th grade, surrounded by other exceptionally bright students. It was refreshing to be in a school where I felt challenged and inspired by my peers. My teachers were amazing. They challenged me in ways I had not experienced in the private school. I remember my 10th grade English class at the private school consisted of a teacher who wanted to be our friend. We never read any literature. We sat and talked about nothing daily. I made straight A's but learned nothing. But in the new school I was placed in honors courses. We read *Beowulf* and other literature with robust discussions about themes and inferences. We wrote term papers where we had to research topics. I felt so behind in my experiences but so excited about this rigorous teaching.

Nervous about being a teen mom in a new school, I feared the judgment of my classmates. However, to my surprise, I discovered that there were other girls in similar situations. This newfound camaraderie provided a sense of belonging and eased my initial anxieties. I forged new friendships, although I couldn't help but miss my old school and the sense of belonging it had provided.

Academically, the journey was not without its challenges. Juggling the demands of school, homework, parenting, and household chores was a monumental task. The expectations in my new family dynamic were different from what I had known with my grandmother. My stepmother, unfamiliar with raising a teenager, introduced stricter rules that added to the pressure.

Matthew 19:26 (NIV)
"Jesus looked at them and said, 'With man this is impossible, but with God all things are possible.'"

Each day, I woke up at 5 a.m. to get Michael dressed before his father picked him up on the days that he went with him. I would then catch a city bus a little after 6 a.m. to arrive at school by 7 a.m. I had never ridden a bus before, and the experience was nerve-wracking due to the presence of strangers. All my classes were Honors, which meant a heavy workload.

The burden of responsibilities took its toll. School ended at 2:15 p.m., and I would rush to the bus to head home. My stepmother greeted me, handing me Michael. I often appeared composed on the outside, but I was secretly falling apart. The facade of having it all together hid the emotional strain I was under. It was a challenging time, and the weight of it all was overwhelming.

Amidst the chaos, there were moments of solace. One night, around 2 a.m., as Michael was fussy, my dad heard us moving around and joined us in our room. He sat with me, offering comfort and conversation while I tended to Michael. These moments of connection provided a lifeline, a reminder that I was not alone on this journey.

Through it all, the presence of my family and the grace of God would prove to be guiding forces that carried me through even the darkest of times.

2 Corinthians 4:8-9 (NIV)
"We are hard pressed on every side, but not crushed; perplexed, but not in despair; persecuted, but not abandoned; struck down, but not destroyed."

My academic journey was a testament to resilience, and it was marked by the invaluable support of scholarships, mentors, and pivotal moments that helped me navigate the path to success.

Within the halls of my school, a guardian angel emerged in the form of a dedicated guidance counselor. She recognized my potential and took me under her wing, providing guidance and support that would prove pivotal in my academic pursuits. She assisted me in securing financial aid, facilitated summer internships, and ensured I remained vigilant about my GPA and ACT scores. Her dedication extended to scholarship applications, ensuring I applied for opportunities that matched my qualifications.

Proverbs 11:14 (NIV)
"For lack of guidance a nation falls, but victory is won through many advisers."

Despite my academic progress, a cloud of conflict loomed over my home life. The responsibilities of motherhood had indeed propelled me into a premature maturity, yet the rules and expectations of childhood continued to govern my actions. This inherent dichotomy between my roles as a mother and a child fostered an environment ripe for discord, ultimately culminating in a painful rupture within our family.

I couldn't help but reflect on my selfish and, at times, childish actions during those turbulent days. Looking back, it was apparent how ungrateful I must have seemed to my father and stepmother. In my youthful eagerness to assert my independence and pursue my own desires, I failed to fully appreciate the immense sacrifices they were making on my behalf.

What did I truly comprehend of the sacrifices my father and stepmother made for me? The financial strain they endured to support my education and provide a stable home for Michael and me was substantial. My stepmother, with her unwavering support, took on the role of a caregiver to ensure that I could continue attending school. The burden they bore, both emotionally and financially, must have been substantial, and my actions did not always reflect the gratitude they deserved.

As I pushed against the boundaries they set, the rift between us grew wider. My desires for a normal teenage life and the freedom to explore my newfound independence clashed with their expectations of me as a responsible daughter and mother. Arguments and tension became an unfortunate part of our daily lives, making our home environment increasingly untenable. This dichotomy resulted in conflicts with my stepmother, ultimately leading to my departure from my dad's house in the middle of the school year.

In the years that followed, I would come to realize the depth of my father's and stepmother's sacrifices and the enduring love that compelled them to support me, even in the face of my youthful obstinacy. It was a lesson in humility and gratitude, one that would shape my understanding of the sacrifices parents make for their children and the profound importance of family bonds.

Ephesians 6:1-4 (NIV)
"Children, obey your parents in the Lord, for this is right. 'Honor your father and mother'—which is the first commandment with a promise—'so that it may go well with you and that you may enjoy a long life on the earth.' Fathers, do not exasperate your children; instead, bring them up in the training and instruction of the Lord."

A New Chapter with My Aunt

My new refuge became my aunt's home, a place where I continued to face challenges but found strength in my growing faith. The responsibilities extended beyond academics; I was now tasked with cooking dinner, babysitting, and assisting her children with school matters. The journey was tough, but it was during this time that I began to recognize the presence of something greater than myself at work—God's guidance.

As I settled into my aunt's home, the stark contrast between my life before and my life now was undeniable. The once familiar routine of attending private school, where I had thrived academically, had been replaced by a world of new responsibilities and uncertainties.

With each passing day, I found myself taking on roles I had never anticipated. Cooking dinner became a nightly task, and while my culinary skills were far from gourmet, I persevered with determination. Babysitting my cousins allowed me to understand the demands of parenthood even better, and I marveled at how my aunt managed to juggle it all.

My birthday has always been an important day of celebration. It marked another year of life, a reminder of the journey I had undertaken and the challenges I had overcome. But one particular birthday would stand out as a poignant memory, etched into the tapestry of my life.

One weekend, my aunt had to work overtime, and the responsibility of taking care of my cousins and Michael fell squarely on my shoulders. Our routine was familiar—errand running, cooking dinner, and spending quality time at home. Sometimes, when my aunt worked late shifts, she would have me pick up leftover food from her job, often filled with delectable desserts and treats. Those moments of indulgence were small but cherished reprieves from the daily grind.

However, that weekend extended into the week, stretching my responsibilities even further. I recall the day when I had to accompany my aunt to her workplace after registering her children for school. At that moment, I felt the weight of my roles pressing down on me—I was not just a teenager, a mother, and a student, but now something like a nanny as well.

The exhaustion, loneliness, and stress had begun to take their toll. My young shoulders were burdened with responsibilities far beyond my years, and I often struggled to find a moment for myself. And to make matters worse, it was my birthday.

Psalm 34:18 (NIV)
"The Lord is close to the brokenhearted and saves those who are crushed in spirit."

As I stood at my aunt's workplace, picking up food as I had done so many times before, I couldn't hold back the tears that welled up in my eyes. The weight of my circumstances had become almost unbearable. I felt a profound sense of invisibility, as though the world had overlooked the fact that it was my special day.

My aunt, perceptive as ever, noticed the tears and the sadness etched across my face. She gently inquired, "What's wrong?" And with a heavy heart, I uttered the words that had been weighing on me, "It's my birthday."

In that moment, I felt seen, heard, and understood. My aunt's response was not grand or extravagant, but it was filled with compassion and love. She offered a reassuring smile and a simple, heartfelt "Happy birthday." It was a small gesture, yet it meant the world to me. It reminded me that even in the midst of my most challenging moments, there were people who cared, who recognized my struggles, and who were there to offer support.

Isaiah 41:10 (NIV)
"So do not fear, for I am with you; do not be dismayed, for I am your God. I will strengthen you and help you; I will uphold you with my righteous right hand."

That birthday, while tinged with the hardships of my daily life, became a testament to the power of love and the presence of God in the midst of adversity. It was a reminder that I was not alone on this journey, that there were unseen hands guiding me through the darkest of times. Little did I know that this moment of vulnerability would serve as a turning point in my path, leading me toward unexpected blessings and opportunities that lay ahead.

My cousins were my companions, my allies in this new chapter of my life. We tackled homework assignments together, and I realized that assisting them with their school matters was not only a responsibility but also an opportunity to share my knowledge and experiences. Through helping them, I deepened my understanding of the subjects I had studied, reinforcing the importance of education in my own life.

In the midst of these daily challenges, I began to turn to my faith for solace and strength. The burdens I carried felt lighter as I sought guidance and support from a higher power. The journey was far from easy, and there were moments when doubt and exhaustion threatened to overwhelm me. Yet, I clung to my growing belief that God was guiding me through this tumultuous period.

Through prayer and reflection, I found comfort in the knowledge that there was a purpose to my struggles. Each obstacle I faced, whether in academics or daily life, was an opportunity for growth and resilience. My aunt's home became a sanctuary where I not only nurtured my academic aspirations but also cultivated my spiritual connection with God.

As I continued to navigate the challenges of motherhood, family responsibilities, and the pursuit of academic success, I held on to the belief that God's guidance was ever-present. Little did I know that these trying times would prepare me for the unpredictable twists and turns that lay ahead in my journey.

I had a strong foundation in the Catholic faith, but it was during these trying times that I learned to recognize God's movements in my life. The burdens I carried began to feel lighter as I witnessed the impact of faith and trust in God's plan. I saw things happen that transcended my own efforts.

Proverbs 3:5-6 (NIV)
"Trust in the Lord with all your heart and lean not on your own understanding; in all your ways submit to him, and he will make your paths straight."

My unwavering determination and faith paved the way for academic success. I graduated from high school with honors and on time—a significant achievement given the hurdles I had faced. The reward for my perseverance was a full scholarship to a private university in Memphis, with a major in pre-med biology.

My future appeared promising, with dreams of a pre-medical education ahead. However, as they say, "Man plans, and God laughs." Little did I know that my journey was about to take an unexpected turn, filled with new challenges and opportunities that would continue to shape my path.

In the chapters that follow, you will witness the ever-unpredictable nature of life's twists and turns. My journey was far from linear, but the lessons learned along the way would prove invaluable as I continued to pursue my dreams and embrace the unknown with unwavering faith.

JEREMIAH 29:12-13 (NIV)

"Then you will call on me and come and pray to me, and I will listen to you. You will seek me and find me when you seek me with all your heart."

Chapter 6: Breaking Stereotypes: Career and Professional Achievements

In college, I embarked on a journey that would challenge societal norms and redefine the expectations placed upon a young, single mother. My determination to pursue education and a career was unwavering, and my faith served as a guiding light through the turbulent waters of change and self-discovery.

Proverbs 16:3 (NIV)
"Commit to the Lord whatever you do, and he will establish your plans."

I started my college journey with a pre-med biology major, fueled by dreams of a career in medicine. However, the demands of balancing school, work, and motherhood soon led me down a different path. By the end of my freshman year, I found myself living

independently in student apartments, with my son Michael by my side.
'

The transition to independent living was both daunting and liberating. I was now responsible not only for my education but also for providing for my son. I worked part-time at a department store, and with the help of financial aid, I managed to pay my rent and supplement our income.

Our modest apartment was sparsely furnished when we first moved in—just a rug and a blanket. Yet, in our eyes, it felt like a palace. We slept together on the floor, our hearts filled with gratitude for the little we had. As if guided by divine intervention, people around us generously donated furniture and items to make our apartment truly feel like home.

Matthew 6:33 (NIV)
"But seek first his kingdom and his righteousness, and all these things will be given to you as well."

My journey continued to evolve as I took on the role of a front desk clerk at a hotel. I juggled work and school, all while striving to be the best mother I could be. Despite the many responsibilities I carried, I couldn't shake the feeling that something was missing from my life—a sense of companionship and love.

I ventured into relationships, searching for love and a sense of completeness. However, my past experiences had left me with a fear of abandonment and a tendency to run from relationships. I believed that if my own mother had left me, who's to say a man wouldn't do the same? This fear led me to make choices that perpetuated a cycle of leaving before I could be left.

Then, in a twist of fate, I met my new neighbor, someone who felt strangely familiar. He had been a student at the same university I attended, and he lived downstairs. Our connection was undeniable, and we soon found ourselves in a relationship. Not long after, I became pregnant with my second child. At 21 years old, with a burgeoning career and dreams of defying societal expectations, I faced the reality of being a single mother of two.

My journey through college and early adulthood was marked by trials and tribulations, but it also held moments of profound growth and realization. I had gone from being a teenage mother to a single mother of two, all while pursuing my education and career aspirations. I was determined to prove society wrong and break free from the stereotypes that had once confined me.

Jeremiah 29:11 (NIV)
"For I know the plans I have for you, declares the Lord, plans for welfare and not for evil, to give you a future and a hope."

As my senior year in college approached, I found myself working with a non-profit organization, sharing my story and knowledge with young girls across the city. We conducted workshops covering various topics, from the challenges of teenage motherhood to sexual health and financial literacy. The experience was eye-opening, and it ignited a passion within me to work with children and make a positive impact on their lives.

I took an education course during my final semester in college, and witnessing Michael's progress in kindergarten, where he transformed from a non-reader to a literate student, filled me with a sense of purpose. I had discovered my calling—to become a teacher and guide young minds toward a brighter future.

Psalm 119:105 (NIV)
"Your word is a lamp for my feet, a light on my path."

Upon graduating with a bachelor's degree in psychology, I immediately began teaching at a local private school. But my journey didn't stop there. Without missing a beat, I enrolled in graduate school to pursue my Master's degree in education.

My career was taking shape, and I was working in a field that aligned with my passion—education. But the road ahead was not without its challenges. Despite my newfound qualifications, the private school offered me a mere $3,000 increase in salary with my Master's degree, leaving me with a total of $28,000.

Diligence and determination, characteristics nurtured by my upbringing and faith, drove me to seek a path that would honor my dedication and the sacrifices I had made on my journey.

And so, I made the decision to take my talents to the public school system, where I would continue to break stereotypes, challenge expectations, and build a future not just for myself but for my children as well. My journey was far from over, and the chapters yet to be written would be filled with resilience, growth, and the pursuit of a dream that defied the odds.

As my journey in education continued, I found myself in a new role as a public school teacher. The challenges were daunting, but the rewards were immeasurable. I embarked on a path that would allow me to impact the lives of countless children, instilling in them not just knowledge but also a thirst for learning, compassion, and the belief that they could achieve greatness.

Proverbs 9:9 (NIV)
"Instruct the wise and they will be wiser still; teach the righteous and they will add to their learning."

I began my teaching career in a small school, taking on the responsibility of educating fourth-grade students. What made this experience truly exceptional was the diversity of my classroom. My students hailed from various races and countries around the world. Among them was a young boy from the Congo, fluent in four languages, and another student from Pakistan, who spoke Farsi. The classroom was a microcosm of the world, brimming with cultural richness, heritage, and a genuine thirst for knowledge.

My role extended beyond just teaching lessons; I became a listening ear and a source of support for my students. They would share their hopes, dreams, and concerns with me, creating a bond that went beyond the confines of the classroom. I cherished every moment of guiding these young minds and witnessing their growth.

Proverbs 22:17-19 (NIV)
"Pay attention and turn your ear to the sayings of the wise; apply your heart to what I teach, for it is pleasing when you keep them in your heart and have all of them ready on your lips."

My second year at the school was unexpectedly short-lived, but I understood that God's plan for me was ever-evolving. I was transferred to one of the finest public elementary schools in downtown Memphis, a place with abundant resources, supportive parents, and a prime location. Here, I would teach various grade levels, moving from fifth grade to second grade and eventually first grade. Little did I know that these diverse teaching experiences would lay the foundation for my future success.

Ecclesiastes 3:1 (NIV)
"There is a time for everything, and a season for every activity under the heavens."

In addition to the standard curriculum, I introduced my students to real-world concepts. One notable project involved teaching them about economics and the structure of business. Together, we launched a t-shirt company, complete with a CEO, human resources department, graphic designers, marketing team, and even a shipping department. The profits generated from this venture funded an unforgettable trip to the space museum in Huntsville, Alabama, creating lasting memories for my students.

Proverbs 3:13-14 (NIV)
"Blessed are those who find wisdom, those who gain understanding, for she is more profitable than silver and yields better returns than gold."

Teaching first-grade students was a unique experience, and I quickly learned the ins and outs of working with children at such a tender age. They taught me that white pants were a risky choice, that hugs were often preferred over high fives (though sometimes not), and that when a child said they needed to use the restroom, it was best to grant them that opportunity without delay. These early teaching experiences were invaluable, shaping my perspective and approach as an educator.

However, I was eager to explore new horizons and engage with older students. I made the transition to a middle school, where I found my stride and a sense of belonging. Teaching sixth, seventh, and eighth graders brought new challenges and opportunities. In addition to my teaching responsibilities, I coached the cheer team, organized grade-level activities and trips, and played a pivotal role in planning school programs and events.

Philippians 2:3 (NIV)
"Do nothing out of selfish ambition or vain conceit. Rather, in humility value others above yourselves."

My love for education was about to take an unexpected turn. I stumbled upon an opportunity—an educational fellowship—that would shape the trajectory of my career in ways I could never have imagined.

Proverbs 3:6 (NIV)
"In all your ways submit to him, and he will make your paths straight."

I took the leap, applied for the fellowship, and prayed earnestly for guidance. The interview process was nerve-wracking, as I faced questions about student data, education policy, and my beliefs in students' abilities. Yet, I persevered, trusting that if it was meant to be, it would be.

Jeremiah 29:12-13 (NIV)
"Then you will call on me and come and pray to me, and I will listen to you. You will seek me and find me when you seek me with all your heart."

The moment of truth arrived with an email notification—I had been accepted into the first Fellowship Cohort. This opportunity opened doors and set me on a course that would lead to where I stand today, armed with knowledge, experience, and a passion to continue making a difference in the lives of students and educators alike.

Isaiah 6:8 (NIV)
"Then I heard the voice of the Lord saying, 'Whom shall I send? And who will go for us?' And I said, 'Here am I. Send me!'

PROVERBS 31:25 (NIV)

"She is clothed with strength and dignity; she can laugh at the days to come."

Chapter 7: Balancing Act: Juggling Motherhood and Career

As I stood at the intersection of motherhood and career, I realized that life was a delicate balancing act, a continuous journey filled with twists and turns. I had embarked on this path with the unwavering determination to provide a bright future for my children, Michael and my youngest, Joshua, and pursue my passion for teaching. What lay ahead were challenges that tested my resolve and shaped me into the woman I had become.

Proverbs 31:25 (NIV)
"She is clothed with strength and dignity; she can laugh at the days to come."

Balancing the responsibilities of a full-time career while being a mother was no small feat. The demands were unrelenting, but I knew I had to find a way to make it work. Here, I want to share some of the strategies and lessons I learned along the way, in the hope that they may be of help to other parents facing similar challenges.

Prioritize and Organize:

Establish clear priorities for your daily tasks. Identify what truly matters and focus your energy on those areas. Use calendars, to-do lists, and organizational tools to stay on top of your commitments.

I remember one particularly hectic day when I had a parent-teacher conference scheduled at the same time as my son Michael's football game. The conference was essential, but I didn't want to miss Michael's game either. It felt like a classic dilemma for a working parent.

At that moment, I realized the importance of prioritizing and organizing my schedule. I quickly reached out to the school to reschedule the conference and ensured I could attend Michael's game. It was a small but significant adjustment that allowed me to fulfill both my professional and parenting responsibilities without feeling overwhelmed. This experience reinforced the wisdom of Proverbs 14:8, reminding me to be prudent in understanding my priorities and making the necessary adjustments to ensure a balanced life.

Set Boundaries:

Setting boundaries became a crucial aspect of my life, especially as I navigated the demanding roles of motherhood and a career. Proverbs 22:28, "Do not move an ancient boundary stone set up by your ancestors," resonated with me as a reminder of the importance of respecting limits and establishing clear boundaries.

There was a time when I found it challenging to say no, often overextending myself at work and in my personal life. I wanted to excel in both areas, but I soon realized that this approach was unsustainable and detrimental to my well-being.

One evening, I had committed to working late on a project at the office, but I had also promised Michael that I would attend his school event. I found myself torn between fulfilling my work obligations and being present for my son. It was a moment of internal conflict.

Remembering the wisdom from Proverbs, I understood that I needed to set clear boundaries to maintain a healthy work-life balance. I communicated with my supervisor, explaining the importance of attending my son's event and proposing an alternative solution for completing the work project.

To my surprise, my supervisor was understanding and supportive of my decision. This experience taught me the value of open communication and setting boundaries. I learned that respecting my own limits didn't hinder my career; instead, it allowed me to be a better, more present parent and a more focused professional.

Proverbs 22:28 served as a reminder that while it's essential to be dedicated to our work and commitments, it's equally vital to preserve the boundaries that protect our well-being and family life.

Lean on Your Support Network:

Proverbs 17:17, "A friend loves at all times, and a brother is born for a time of adversity," reminds us of the importance of relying on our support network during challenging times. This verse resonated deeply with me during a particular period when I was pursuing my Master's Degree while juggling the responsibilities of motherhood and a career.

As I delved into the rigorous demands of graduate school, I found myself faced with a dilemma. I had to dedicate a substantial amount of time to my studies, leaving me concerned about who would care for Michael and my younger son, Josh, during my long hours at the university.

It was during this challenging period that my younger sister stepped in as a source of unwavering support. She understood the demands of my academic pursuits and the responsibilities of being a mother. Despite being a student herself, she selflessly offered to babysit Michael and Josh during the evenings and weekends when I had classes and assignments to complete.

My sister's willingness to help me during this time exemplified the essence of true friendship and familial love. She became a lifeline for me, allowing me to focus on my studies without the constant worry of childcare.

Proverbs 17:17 teaches us that friends and family are invaluable treasures during times of adversity. They offer their love and support when we need it most, allowing us to navigate the challenges of motherhood and a career with a greater sense of assurance and balance.

Quality Over Quantity:

Proverbs 15:16, "Better a little with the fear of the Lord than great wealth with turmoil," serves as a poignant reminder that the quality of our time with our children far surpasses the quantity of moments spent together. This principle became especially evident in my life during a period when I was balancing the demands of a career and motherhood.

At one point in my journey, my professional responsibilities intensified, demanding more of my time and energy. I found myself facing longer work hours and additional responsibilities that left me with limited free time to spend with my children, Michael and Josh.

Despite the challenges, I made a conscious decision to prioritize quality over quantity when it came to our moments together. I realized that it wasn't about the number of hours I could spend with them but the impact of those hours on their growth and development.

One specific incident etched this lesson into my heart. I had a particularly demanding week at work, with important deadlines and meetings that required my attention. Yet, I was determined to make the most of the precious time I had with Michael and Josh.

One evening, instead of succumbing to the exhaustion from my workday, I decided to engage in a simple but meaningful activity with them. We gathered around the kitchen table, each armed with pizza ingredients, and embarked on a creative adventure of making our own personal pizzas. Our laughter filled the room as we let our imaginations run wild on our culinary arts.

At that moment, I realized the profound truth of Proverbs 15:16. While I couldn't always provide an abundance of time, I could ensure that the time we did spend together was filled with love, joy, and cherished memories. Our food-filled evening was a testament to the power of quality over quantity, and it strengthened our bond as a family.

This verse serves as a gentle reminder to all parents facing the challenge of balancing a career and motherhood that it's the meaningful moments we share with our children that leave a lasting impact, far more than the quantity of time we can offer.

Self-Care Is Essential:

1 Corinthians 6:19-20, "Do you not know that your bodies are temples of the Holy Spirit, who is in you, whom you have received from God? You are not your own," is a powerful reminder of the importance of self-care. It underscores the idea that we are entrusted with our bodies and must care for them to honor the divine gift of life.

During a particularly hectic period in my life, as I juggled the responsibilities of a demanding career and the challenges of motherhood, I learned the significance of self-care in a profoundly personal way. The demands of my profession had increased, and I found myself constantly on the move, attending meetings, managing my classroom, and supporting my students.

In the midst of this whirlwind, I began to neglect my own well-being. I wasn't eating healthy meals, sacrificed sleep, and rarely took a moment to pause and breathe. I was giving my all to my career and my children, but I was neglecting the temple of my own body.

One day, a close friend invited me to join her for a kick-boxing class. It was a simple invitation, but it held the promise of something transformative. I decided to take a break from my hectic routine and join her at the gym.

As we jabbed at imaginary threats, surrounded by bass thumping hip hop beats, I felt a profound sense of peace and rejuvenation. The verse from 1 Corinthians 6:19-20 echoed in my mind, reminding me that my body was indeed a temple, a sacred vessel that deserved care and attention.

During that class, I realized that self-care wasn't a luxury but a necessity. It was a way to honor the divine presence within me and ensure that I had the physical and emotional strength to continue fulfilling my roles as a mother and a professional.

From that day forward, I made self-care a non-negotiable part of my routine. Whether it was going to a beauty shop, a few moments of meditation, or simply enjoying a quiet cup of hot chocolate, I recognized that taking care of myself was not selfish but an act of stewardship over the temple I had been entrusted with.

This experience taught me that when we neglect self-care, we compromise our ability to fulfill our roles effectively and with love. It's a lesson I carry with me, a reminder that taking care of ourselves is an essential aspect of our journey as parents and professionals.

Open Communication:

Proverbs 21:23, "Those who guard their mouths and their tongues keep themselves from calamity," speaks to the wisdom of thoughtful communication. It reminds us that when we communicate openly and honestly, we can avoid unnecessary conflicts and misunderstandings.

In my journey as a working mother, I encountered a situation where open communication played a pivotal role in maintaining a healthy balance between my career and family life.

I had recently transitioned to a new role within my school district, one that came with increased responsibilities and expectations. While I was excited about the opportunity, I knew that it would require a more demanding schedule and occasional after-hours commitments.

Around the same time, my youngest son, Josh, was facing some challenges in school that required additional attention and support. It was a delicate balance, as I didn't want my commitment to my job to compromise the support and presence I could provide for him at home.

One evening, I found myself facing a significant work-related event that coincided with an important parent-teacher meeting for Josh. It was a dilemma that weighed heavily on my mind. I couldn't help but feel torn between my responsibilities as a mother and my commitment to my classroom.In my journey through the education system, I gained an even deeper appreciation for the importance of teachers and the challenges they faced. As teachers we learned quickly that missing school was frowned upon, even when we had valid reasons. It was a profession that demanded unwavering commitment, with little room for personal time or sick days.

In the midst of this internal struggle, I remembered the wisdom of Proverbs 21:23. I realized that guarding my tongue and keeping my concerns to myself would only lead to increased stress and potential calamity. It was time to communicate openly with my principal.

The next morning, I scheduled a meeting with my principal to discuss the situation honestly and transparently. I expressed my dedication to my job and my commitment to supporting my son's education. I was pleasantly surprised by my principal's response.

Rather than viewing my situation as a conflict, my principal appreciated my openness and commitment to both my family and my career. Together, we explored potential solutions, such as flexible use of my planning period and before school hours.

This open dialogue allowed us to find a compromise that benefited everyone involved. I could tend to my son's needs while still fulfilling my work obligations effectively. The sense of understanding and support from my employer made all the difference in maintaining a healthy work-life balance.

This experience taught me that open communication is not a sign of weakness but a demonstration of wisdom and strength. It's a reminder that when we express our needs and challenges honestly, we create opportunities for understanding, empathy, and collaborative solutions that benefit both our families and our careers.

Celebrate Milestones:

Psalm 127:3 beautifully reminds us that "Children are a heritage from the Lord, offspring a reward from him." This verse emphasizes the preciousness of our children and the joy they bring into our lives. It also serves as a reminder to celebrate the milestones, both big and small, in our roles as parents and professionals.

In my journey as a working mother, I've come to understand the importance of celebrating these milestones, as they serve as moments of reflection, motivation, and gratitude.

One Mother's Day, while working full-time as a middle school teacher, I faced an incredibly challenging semester. The demands of coaching, teaching, and parenting had reached an all-time high. I felt like I was constantly juggling multiple responsibilities, and the stress was taking its toll.

During this hectic period, I made a commitment to myself to maintain a sense of balance and to acknowledge and celebrate both my personal and professional achievements, no matter how small they might seem.

I used this moment as an opportunity to express my gratitude to my boys for their patience and understanding during this challenging time. I told them how proud I was of their resilience and the amazing young men they were becoming. We talked about the importance of education, hard work, and the value of perseverance in pursuing one's dreams.

To my surprise, my sons responded with their own words of encouragement and pride in my achievements. They shared stories of how they looked up to me as a role model, not just as their mother but as someone who was determined and dedicated to her goals.

In that moment, I realized the profound impact our celebrations of milestones can have on our families. It was not only a moment of recognizing my own accomplishments but also an opportunity to strengthen the bond with my children and teach them the importance of acknowledging and celebrating their successes, no matter how small.

As time went on, we continued to celebrate our achievements, whether it was finishing a challenging project at work or reaching a new academic milestone. These moments of celebration became an integral part of our family life, fostering a sense of unity, gratitude, and motivation.

Psalm 127:3 reminds us that our children are a gift and a reward, and celebrating our accomplishments as parents and professionals is a way of cherishing and honoring that gift. It teaches us that in the midst of life's challenges and busy schedules, taking time to celebrate the journey and the people we share it with is a precious and enriching experience.

Learn to Forgive Yourself:
As a young parent, I embarked on the journey of motherhood with boundless love and determination, coupled with a healthy dose of naivety. It wasn't long before I realized that the pursuit of perfection was an elusive goal. Reflecting on my journey, I've come to

acknowledge the mistakes I made while raising my son, Michael – mistakes that left an impact and created unintentional trauma for him, just as my relatives' actions had done to me.

Looking back, I can see that many of the decisions I made were not in Michael's best interest or conducive to nurturing his young and growing mind. I inadvertently etched traces of trauma onto his canvas of life, much like the generational baggage I carried from those who came before me. It's a sobering realization that, as parents, we bring our raw, imperfect selves into the role, often unknowingly perpetuating the pain of our past.

What did I know back then? What could I have understood about how our own experiences and struggles as parents could leave indelible marks on our children? It's a complex and often uncharted territory, one that requires introspection, forgiveness – both of ourselves and those who came before us – and a commitment to breaking the cycle of trauma, ultimately creating a brighter and healthier future for our children.

One particularly challenging day, as I was immersed in my responsibilities as a mother and a teacher, a vivid incident occurred that forever etched the importance of self-forgiveness in my heart.

I had just finished a long day at school, where I had faced the constant demands of a classroom full of eager young minds. The weight of my responsibilities as a mother and educator had worn me down, leaving me feeling depleted. It was one of those days when exhaustion seemed to seep into my very core.

As I returned home, I yearned for a moment of respite. However, my younger son, Josh, had been eagerly awaiting my arrival. He had an upcoming school project and needed my assistance. Overwhelmed by the mounting pressures of work and motherhood, I found myself snapping at Josh, my impatience spilling over.

Seeing the hurt in his eyes and the quiver in his voice, I was overcome with guilt and regret. I had let my exhaustion and frustration get the best of me, and it had hurt someone I loved dearly. I immediately hugged Josh, apologizing for my outburst and explaining that I was tired and stressed but that it was no excuse for how I had treated him.

That evening, as I lay in bed, I reflected on my actions. I realized that I had allowed the relentless balancing act of motherhood and career to consume me, to the detriment of my own well-being and those around me. I turned to the comforting words of 1 John 1:9, which reminded me of the importance of seeking forgiveness and cleansing my spirit of unrighteousness.

I asked Josh for forgiveness once more, and he forgave me with the forgiving heart of a child. As I reflect on my journey as an ever evolving parent, the most crucial step has been forgiving myself. I understood that I was not perfect, and mistakes were an inevitable part of life. What mattered was how I learned from them and grew as a mother and a person.

These experiences and reflections serve as a poignant reminder that self-forgiveness has been an essential aspect of the delicate balance between motherhood and a career. It allowed me to release the burden of guilt, offering a chance for redemption and personal growth. With this newfound understanding, I continue my journey, striving to be the best mother and educator I could be while remembering to extend grace and forgiveness, both to others and to myself.

"One who has unreliable friends soon comes to ruin, but there is a friend who sticks closer than a brother."

PROVERBS 18:24 (NIV)

Chapter 8: Building a Support System: Friendships and Relationships

Throughout the winding journey of my life, there have been constant companions and pillars of strength that have played pivotal roles in shaping my path. In this chapter, we delve into the importance of building a support system through friendships and relationships – the bonds that have sustained me through various trials and triumphs.

Proverbs 18:24 (NIV) - "One who has unreliable friends soon comes to ruin, but there is a friend who sticks closer than a brother."

My journey through high school was far from ordinary, marked by the responsibilities of motherhood and the pursuit of academic excellence. Amidst the complexities of those years, a steadfast friend emerged, one who would prove to be a lifelong companion. From high school to college and into adulthood, our friendship has been a source of unwavering support.

An Unbreakable Bond: My Best Friend

In high school, I was blessed to meet a kindred spirit, a friend who would walk beside me through thick and thin. We shared dreams and aspirations, but more importantly, we shared the burdens of not having our mothers in our lives while growing up. Our friendship was a sanctuary of understanding, where we could confide in one another without judgment. As a young mother navigating the turbulent waters of adolescence, I leaned on her shoulders, as she provided strength when it was needed most without judgment.

Through countless late-night conversations, shared laughter, and tears shed together, our bond only grew stronger. My best friend was not just a confidant but a co-conspirator in our pursuit of a better life for ourselves. She believed in me when I doubted myself and encouraged me to keep pushing forward, and vice versa.

College Years: A Test of Friendship

As we ventured into college, our paths and our friendship remained steadfast. We attended the same private university, both pursuing our degrees in Pre-Med Biology. We attended classes together daily. We were inseparable. We worked the same jobs and at one point we even had the same car.

Ecclesiastes 4:9-10 (NIV) - "Two are better than one, because they have a good return for their labor: If either of them falls down, one can help the other up. But pity anyone who falls and has no one to help them up."

In college, where the academic demands were even more demanding, our bond proved invaluable. We embodied the idea that "two are better than one," as our combined efforts and shared experiences enriched our education. When one of us stumbled academically or faced personal challenges, the other was there to lift them up, fulfilling the promise of Ecclesiastes. Our experiences in college were profound, as we both navigated the rigorous academic demands of Pre-Med Biology. It was a time when our friendship was tested, and we emerged even stronger. We studied together, celebrated our successes, and provided unwavering support during challenging times.

Our connection extended beyond the classroom, transcending into the fabric of our lives. We were not just friends; we were each other's confidants, cheerleaders, and partners in the pursuit of a brighter future.

As we continue to journey through life, our friendship remains a testament to the enduring truth of these verses. We have found that having a loyal friend who sticks closer than a brother is a blessing beyond measure. Our shared experiences and unwavering support are a testament to the wisdom found in the Book of Ecclesiastes.

Adulting Together: A Lifelong Connection

As we transitioned into adulthood, our friendship only deepened. We faced the trials of career and parenthood together, providing a constant source of encouragement and understanding. We celebrated birthdays, milestones, and the everyday victories that life had to offer.

Through the years, our friendship remained a testament to the power of unwavering support and the bond that is forged through shared experiences. We grew individually, but our connection remained unchanged, a source of solace and inspiration.

This friendship played a pivotal role in shaping my life and the lives of those around me, offering guidance, strength, and an enduring sense of belonging. We have celebrated each other's successes and provided solace during moments of doubt and despair.

A Crew of Friends: A Strong Social Network

During my tenure as a teacher, particularly at the middle school where I worked, I found myself surrounded by a remarkable crew of friends and colleagues who played a pivotal role in my life. This dynamic group of colleagues who soon became more than just coworkers – they became a cherished crew of friends, family. We shared the joys and challenges of teaching, creating a bond that extended beyond the classroom.This group of individuals embodied the essence of teamwork and support, standing by my side through thick and thin.

Our collective experiences as educators provided a unique perspective and a deep well of empathy. We supported each other through the demands of the profession, lending a listening ear and offering guidance during both professional and personal challenges. As a fellow teacher, cheer coach, and activity sponsor, my responsibilities extended far beyond the classroom. I was involved in various aspects of school life, from organizing events to managing school programs. It was a demanding role that required dedication and tireless effort.

Proverbs 27:9 (NIV) beautifully states, "Perfume and incense bring joy to the heart, and the pleasantness of a friend springs from their heartfelt advice." In the midst of these demanding responsibilities, my friends provided the sweet fragrance of support and camaraderie. Their heartfelt advice and unwavering presence brought joy to my heart.

One remarkable chapter in our journey together was the school trip to Disney World, a week-long adventure that required meticulous planning and tireless chaperoning. My friends stepped up without hesitation, joining me in ensuring the safety and enjoyment of our students. We created lasting memories for our students, and their dedication exemplified the essence of Proverbs 27:17 (NIV): "As iron sharpens iron, so one person sharpens another." We strengthened each other, both personally and professionally, throughout this memorable experience.

Another significant undertaking was the school pageant production. From organizing auditions to coordinating rehearsals, costume fittings, and the final performance, the task was immense. My friends selflessly devoted their time and effort, working tirelessly behind the scenes to make the production a resounding success. Their support and commitment demonstrated the truth of Ecclesiastes 4:12 (NIV): "Though one may be overpowered, two can defend themselves. A cord of three strands is not quickly broken." Our combined efforts made us stronger, ensuring the success of the pageant.

Through the ups and downs of my career, these friends became my pillars of strength, demonstrating the significance of having a support system in the workplace. Just as Ecclesiastes 4:9-10 (NIV) states, "Two are better than one, because they have a good return for their labor: If either of them falls down, one can help the other up." In our case, it was a team effort, and we lifted each other up in both our personal and professional lives.

My group of friends, whom I affectionately call "Black Girl Magic," has been an invaluable support system and source of strength throughout my journey. We first came together during our time at the last school where I taught, and from the very beginning, our bond was unbreakable. These incredible women, each a shining example of resilience, perseverance, and excellence, have been my sounding board and sanctuary.

We were not just colleagues; we were a close-knit sisterhood. We leaned on each other during the most challenging of days, whether it was the trials of motherhood, navigating complex relationships, or the demands of our roles as educators. Our gatherings were a lifeline, moments of respite where we could let our hair down, laugh, cry, and simply be ourselves.

From entertaining at each other's homes to indulging in brunch outings, we found solace in each other's company, knowing that we could openly share our triumphs and tribulations. These women embodied the essence of "Black Girl Magic," and together, we proved that strength, resilience, and friendship know no bounds. They have been my pillars of support, and I am eternally grateful for their presence in my life.

The invaluable friendships and bonds formed during these years are a testament to the power of support. They remind me that even in the midst of life's challenges, we can find strength and joy in the company of friends who stand by our side.

These friendships were not just about camaraderie; they were a source of inspiration and growth. We learned from each other, shared our wisdom, and provided strength during times of uncertainty. Together, we forged a tight-knit community that extended beyond the workplace, creating bonds that would last a lifetime.

JEREMIAH 29:11 (NIV)

"For I know the plans I have for you," declares the Lord, "plans to prosper you and not to harm you, plans to give you hope and a future."

Chapter 9: Trials and Triumphs: Overcoming Adversity

Life is a journey filled with twists and turns, trials and triumphs. In this chapter, I invite you to walk with me through some of the most challenging moments I've encountered, both personally and professionally, and how the power of resilience and a determined mindset guided me through these adversities.

Life has a way of throwing unexpected storms our way. Just when I thought I was finding my footing in my career, a professional challenge of immense magnitude arose. I was content where I worked. My co-workers had become my family. I enjoyed coaching cheer. I knew the parents and lived in the community where I taught. But then, it happened – a sudden change that seemed almost divine in its timing.

"For I know the plans I have for you," declares the Lord, "plans to prosper you and not to harm you, plans to give you hope and a future." - Jeremiah 29:11 (NIV)

I received a phone call from a principal at another school during cheer practice one afternoon during the summer. Before I interviewed, I couldn't figure out how the principal accessed me from the transfer pool. Shortly after my interview I received news that I had been chosen, I transferred to another middle school in the suburbs. It was as if God's hand was guiding me towards this new opportunity, even though I couldn't fully comprehend it at the time. Change can be daunting, especially when we've grown comfortable in our current circumstances. But I knew that sometimes God makes you move, even when you don't think it's time, and in those moments, we must be obedient.

"Your word is a lamp for my feet, a light on my path." - Psalm 119:105 (NIV)

I accepted the new position, and with a heavy heart, I bid farewell to the school, the students, and the community I had come to love. I wasn't sure what lay ahead, but I had faith that this unexpected change held a purpose, even if I couldn't see it clearly.

"Trust in the Lord with all your heart and lean not on your own understanding; in all your ways submit to him, and he will make your paths straight." - Proverbs 3:5-6 (NIV)

As I ventured into this new chapter, my son, Joshua, accompanied me to the new school. Together, we faced the uncertainty, leaning on our faith and trusting that God's plan would reveal itself in due time. Little did I know that this storm would lead to unforeseen opportunities and blessings that would shape the course of my life in profound ways.

The Balancing Act

Balancing the demands of motherhood and a thriving career was an ongoing challenge that intensified with time. By this point, I had two additional little ones in tow, and yes, that meant managing the care and well-being of four kids! The logistics of living in one part of the city while Michael attended school in another, with Joshua's activities also in yet another area, created a web of stress that at times felt almost suffocating. But amidst the chaos, I clung to the belief that being a dedicated mother and pursuing a fulfilling career could coexist harmoniously; they did not have to be at odds with each other. It was a matter of finding that elusive equilibrium that would enable me to give my best in both realms.

"I can do all things through him who strengthens me." - Philippians 4:13 (NIV)

Strategic planning became my guiding star in navigating this intricate terrain. I meticulously structured my days, ensuring that the diverse needs of my family and career were given their due attention. It was a challenging endeavor, and there were moments of doubt and exhaustion, but I pressed forward with unwavering determination.

Open communication was a vital tool in my mission to strike a balance between motherhood and career. I maintained transparent dialogue with my colleagues and superiors, ensuring they were well aware of my responsibilities as a parent. This honesty fostered an environment of understanding and support, proving invaluable during moments of unforeseen challenges.

To facilitate this equilibrium, I made a significant decision to sell my house and relocate to a rental closer to the school. This shift drastically reduced the logistical complexity, as the younger ones were now able to attend daycare near their school. Meanwhile, Michael graduated and was on his way to college, a proud moment that symbolized the successful balancing act I had orchestrated.

The relentless challenge of harmonizing motherhood and career persisted, but through unwavering determination, strategic planning, and open communication, I managed to find a balance that allowed me to thrive in both roles.

With God as my anchor, I had weathered this storm, proving that the relentless challenge of the balancing act could indeed be conquered, paving the way for fulfillment and success on both fronts.

Personal Loss

Life can be both a source of boundless joy and an arena for heart-wrenching blows. The loss of a loved one, particularly my beloved grandmother, Ma, was one such devastating moment etched into the tapestry of my life. She battled with lung cancer, a cruel adversary that seemed to consume her in less than a year. Witnessing her journey through this relentless disease was a painful experience, one that left an indelible mark on my heart.

The simple tasks of life became monumental challenges for Ma as her condition deteriorated. I can vividly recall one holiday when she was in the kitchen, her favorite pastime, attempting to cook. In those moments, even the act of breathing had become a struggle. She would stand at the stove, her frail form silhouetted against the soft glow of the kitchen lights, and every few minutes, she'd sit down to catch her breath. It was agonizing to watch her decline, to witness a woman who had once been a powerful presence reduced to a mere shadow of her former self.

As her condition worsened, her medications aimed at providing comfort sometimes had unexpected effects. She would nod off, only to awaken in a state of confusion. On those nights, I slept on the couch right beside her bed, ready to provide reassurance and a comforting presence.

Despite the physical toll that her illness exacted, Ma never lost her dry humor and sharp wit. Her medications often caused her to drift in and out of sleep, occasionally plunging her into surreal hallucinations. She confided in my aunt and me, asking us to stay with her overnight to help distinguish between reality and her vivid dreams. I remember one night, we were both asleep, and she abruptly awoke with a start, blurting out an expletive. Startled, I asked her what was wrong, and she replied, "I'm still here!" We shared a heartfelt laugh, even in the face of her impending departure, finding solace in the enduring bond of our humor. I can still recall the moments when her face would light up with laughter or when she'd share her mischievous sense of humor, despite the circumstances.

Ma's passing left a void that felt impossible to fill. Grief and sorrow threatened to engulf me, and the weight of her absence pressed down on my soul. It took me three long months before I could summon the courage to set foot in her house. The realization that she would no longer be there to unlock the door, or answer when I called her name as I entered, was a devastating blow. I sat in the driveway for what felt like an eternity, tears flowing uncontrollably, my anguish escaping through my eyes. My best friend, ever the steadfast companion, answered my call and simply listened as I cried. Words could not convey the depth of my grief, but her presence on the other end of the line was a lifeline of comfort. I remember the particularly painful day when I turned the key in the lock, walked into the silent house, and called out her name, only to be met with an agonizing silence. When I longed to hear her voice I would call her cell phone and listen to her voicemail message. On repeat.

I tried to be strong, just as Ma had asked us to. But the essence of her had departed, leaving behind a hollow emptiness. Her scent was gone, her spirit no longer lingered in the corners of the rooms she had inhabited for so long. The house felt empty, devoid of the woman who had filled it with love and life. I clung to the memories we had created together, the invaluable lessons she had imparted, and the boundless love she had showered upon me.

"Blessed are those who mourn, for they will be comforted." - Matthew 5:4 (NIV)

Her legacy became a guiding light in the midst of my grief, a testament to the enduring power of love and the profound impact one person can have on another's life. I found solace in the knowledge that her spirit lived on within me, and that I could carry forward the wisdom and strength she had bestowed upon me, ensuring that her memory would remain an eternal source of inspiration.

The Power of Resilience

Throughout my life, I have come to understand the profound impact that resilience can have on our personal journeys. Resilience is not just about bouncing back from adversity; it's about finding the strength within ourselves to heal, grow, and transform. One of the most powerful demonstrations of resilience in my life has been the renewal of my relationship with my mother, a journey that has taught me the true meaning of forgiveness, redemption, and the importance of embracing second chances.

For many years, my mother's absence had cast a long shadow over my life. Her struggles with addiction had left wounds that ran deep, and the pain of her absence had fueled my determination to prove my worth. I often wondered what was so wrong with me that she couldn't be there for me when I needed her most. It was a question that gnawed at my self-esteem, but it was also a question that would ultimately lead to one of the most profound transformations in my life.

The story of the prodigal son, found in the Bible in the book of Luke 15:11-32, resonates deeply with my own journey. In this parable, a wayward son leaves home, squanders his inheritance, and finds himself in dire circumstances. When he returns to his father, broken and repentant, he is welcomed with open arms and celebration. It is a story of forgiveness, redemption, and the power of love to heal old wounds.

In a similar way, my mother embarked on her own journey of redemption. Over two decades ago, she made the courageous decision to confront her addiction and seek sobriety. It was not an easy path, and there were many challenges along the way. But as time passed, she proved her commitment to change, and her transformation was nothing short of miraculous.

The process of rebuilding our relationship was not without its struggles. Forgiveness, I learned, is a complex and multifaceted journey. It required me to release the anger and resentment that had built up over the years and to open my heart to the possibility of healing. It meant letting go of the past and embracing the present with an open mind and a compassionate spirit.

As my mother continued on her path, our relationship began to evolve. We embarked on a journey of healing old wounds and creating new memories together. It was a process that required patience, understanding, and a willingness to let go of the past.

Over time, our renewed relationship blossomed into something beautiful and profound. My mother became a source of inspiration and strength, and I found myself learning valuable lessons from her journey of life. Her resilience, determination, and unwavering faith were a testament to the power of the human spirit to overcome adversity.

Today, as I reflect on our renewed relationship, I am reminded of the prodigal son's return to his father's embrace. In my mother's return to the fold of our family, I have witnessed the transformative power of love, forgiveness, and the unwavering belief in the potential for redemption.

Our story serves as a reminder that resilience is not just about bouncing back; it's about the capacity to heal, grow, and rebuild even stronger than before. It is a testament to the enduring power of forgiveness and the ability to create new beginnings, no matter how challenging the past may have been.

The journey of resilience has not only shaped my life but has also allowed me to witness the remarkable transformation of my mother. Together, we have created a renewed relationship built on love, forgiveness, and the belief in second chances. It is a testament to the enduring power of the human spirit to overcome adversity and find redemption in the most unexpected places.

Through every twist and turn, every test and trial, resilience became my most cherished companion. It was the unwavering belief that, no matter how formidable the challenges life presented, I possessed the inner strength to surmount them. It was the understanding that each obstacle held the potential for growth and transformation. It was the unwavering conviction that I could overcome any adversity, time and time again.

As my journey continued, I found myself in a position that pushed me to my limits. It was my last year at the new school, and I was entrusted with a unique challenge. My principal asked me to teach a group of students who needed not just education, but an extra dose of love and support. What made this task particularly daunting was the unconventional approach we were taking with these middle school students. They were to be taught Math, Science, History, and Reading all by me, a situation unheard of for students of their age. The weight of this responsibility began to take a toll on my health, both physically and mentally.

One day, I visited my doctor, and the news was grim. My blood pressure had reached a level that posed a severe risk of a stroke. My doctor's words were a wake-up call, a stark reminder that we are not given new bodies, and the toll of stress can be insurmountable. I knew I needed to make a change, and the search for a new job in education began.

Amidst the sea of job listings, one position caught my attention. I decided to take a leap of faith and applied for it, thinking it was a long shot. The application process was arduous, filled with performance tasks that tested my mettle. Yet, my years of experience in and out of the classroom gave me the resilience to persevere. Against the odds, I continued progressing to the next round, each step drawing me closer to a potential new opportunity.

But I couldn't help but wonder if I was truly meant to be there. It was then that I turned to prayer, seeking guidance and strength from God. I knew that if this path was meant for me, I would keep moving forward.

Round after round, I triumphed over the challenges presented, proving to myself that even in the face of adversity, I could rise. The final interview was a test of my abilities, including a role-play scenario and the crucial question of salary expectations. At that time, my teacher's salary was $55,000, a respectable figure. But with the addition of four children to my life, finances had become tight. So, I boldly requested a salary of $76,000.

I left the interview with bated breath, my future hanging in the balance. But the call came sooner than I expected, and their offer left me stunned. They didn't just offer me the job; they welcomed me with open arms to a role as a Director of School Support, an instructional leadership coach, at a salary of $80,000 a year. It was a transformation I had not seen coming, a testament to the power of faith, resilience, and unwavering obedience.

Today, I am still with the company, now in the role of Senior Director and earning a six-figure income. I've even started my own Educational Consulting Business. I couldn't help but think of Ma and how far I had come since the days of hardship and adversity.

"And after you have suffered a little while, the God of all grace, who has called you to his eternal glory in Christ, will himself restore, confirm, strengthen, and establish you." - 1 Peter 5:10 (NIV)

I couldn't help but marvel at the twists and turns life had thrown my way, and how each challenge had ultimately shaped me into the person I had become. Through faith, determination, and the power of resilience, I had not only weathered the storms but emerged stronger and more resilient than ever.

"Train up a child in the way he should go; even when he is old, he will not depart from it."

PROVERBS
22:6 (NIV)

Chapter 10: Lessons for the Next Generation: Parenting and Mentorship

As I look back on the incredible journey, filled with trials and triumphs, one of the most profound roles I have taken on is that of a parent and a mentor. These roles have been the cornerstones of my existence, shaping the person I am today and guiding me toward a future filled with purpose and meaning.

A Journey of Parenting

My journey into motherhood was not one I anticipated at a young age, but it became a defining chapter of my life. The responsibilities of raising a child at the tender age of fifteen forced me to mature quickly, navigate uncharted waters, and develop unwavering determination. It was a journey filled with uncertainty, sleepless nights, and a relentless pursuit of a brighter future.

"Train up a child in the way he should go; even when he is old, he will not depart from it." - Proverbs 22:6 (NIV)

My children became my greatest teachers. Their presence in my life challenged me to become the best version of myself. Through the ups and downs, I learned the importance of resilience, faith, and unwavering love. It was not a smooth path, and I made my fair share of mistakes. However, I realized that perfection was an elusive goal, and what truly mattered was the love and support I provided to my children.

The importance of instilling values and faith in my children became clear to me. I wanted them to grow up with a strong moral compass, guided by principles of kindness, empathy, and perseverance. My faith in God played a significant role in shaping their upbringing. I wanted them to understand that, through faith, they could overcome any obstacle and find strength in times of adversity.

Passing the Torch of Mentorship

My own journey as a young mother navigating the challenges of life without a maternal figure's constant presence left me with a burning desire to guide and support other young mothers facing similar struggles. I knew the importance of mentorship, of having someone who had walked a similar path and could provide guidance and understanding.

It was during my time as a teacher and cheerleading coach that I had the privilege of mentoring young girls and mothers alike. I shared my story, my triumphs, and my failures, letting them know that they were not alone in their journey. Through workshops, open conversations, and unwavering support, I became an advocate for young mothers, empowering them to break free from the cycle of adversity and reach for a brighter future.

As a mentor, I emphasized the importance of education, self-respect, and self-care. I wanted these young mothers to understand that they were capable of achieving their dreams, no matter their circumstances. I encouraged them to lean on their faith, just as I had, and find strength in their resilience.

A Legacy of Love and Guidance

Today, as I reflect on my own parenting journey and my role as a mentor, I am filled with a profound sense of gratitude. My children have grown into strong, compassionate individuals, guided by the values and faith we instilled in them. They have become a source of inspiration and pride, a testament to the enduring power of love and resilience.

As I continue to mentor and advocate for young mothers, I am reminded of the importance of passing on the torch of guidance and support. It is a legacy of love and resilience that I hope will inspire future generations to overcome adversity, find strength in their faith, and embrace the boundless potential that lies within them.

The journey of parenting and mentorship is a continuous one, filled with lessons and blessings. Through it all, I have learned that with faith, determination, and unwavering love, we can shape not only our own lives but also the lives of those who follow in our footsteps. And as we pass on the lessons learned, we create a brighter and more hopeful future for the next generation.

"And we know that in all things God works for the good of those who love him, who have been called according to his purpose."

ROMANS 8:28 (NIV)

Epilogue: Looking Back and Moving Forward

As I sit down to reflect on the journey of my life, I am reminded of the countless experiences that have shaped me into the person I am today. Through the highs and lows, the unexpected storms, and the moments of immense joy, I have come to understand the profound power of faith, resilience, and unwavering love.

Romans 8:28 (NIV) - "And we know that in all things God works for the good of those who love him, who have been called according to his purpose."

Key Takeaways

Throughout my life, I have learned invaluable lessons that continue to guide me on my path:

Faith Can Move Mountains: In the face of adversity, my faith in God has been my unwavering anchor. It is through faith that I found the strength to overcome obstacles, embrace resilience, and navigate life's challenges.

Resilience Is a Lifelong Companion: Trials and tribulations are a part of life's journey. It is our resilience, our ability to rise above adversity, that defines us. With determination and faith, we can weather any storm.

Family Is a Precious Gift: Family, whether biological or chosen, holds a special place in our hearts. The love and support of my grandmother, Ma, and my children have been my greatest blessings, reminding me of the importance of love, sacrifice, and connection.

Mentorship Shapes Lives: As a mentor and advocate, I have witnessed the transformative power of guidance and support. It is our duty to pass on our wisdom and love to the next generation, empowering them to reach for their dreams.

Balance Is Achievable: Balancing the demands of motherhood and a career is a challenge, but it is possible. Through strategic planning, open communication, and unwavering determination, we can flourish in both roles.

Hopes and Aspirations for the Future

As I look to the future, my hopes and aspirations are rooted in the values and lessons I have learned throughout my life's journey:

To Continue Inspiring: I aspire to continue inspiring others through my story, my mentorship, and my advocacy. I want to be a source of hope and encouragement for those facing adversity, reminding them that they possess the strength to overcome.

To Foster Resilient Generations: My greatest wish is to pass on the legacy of resilience, faith, and unwavering love to my children and future generations. I hope to instill in them the belief that they can overcome any challenge and make a positive impact on the world.

To Embrace New Challenges: Life is ever-evolving, and I am eager to embrace new challenges and opportunities that come my way. With faith as my guide, I will continue to grow, learn, and adapt to whatever the future holds.

To Leave a Legacy of Love: Ultimately, I want my legacy to be one of love. I hope to be remembered as someone who loved unconditionally, who supported others in their journey, and who left the world a little brighter through acts of kindness and compassion.

In closing, I am reminded of the verse from Romans 8:28, which speaks to the idea that all things work together for the good of those who love God and are called according to His purpose. My life's journey has been a testament to this truth, and as I move forward, I do so with gratitude for the past, faith in the present, and hope for the future. With God's guidance, I am ready to face whatever lies ahead and continue to make a positive impact on the world around me.

"And after you have suffered a little while, the God of all grace, who has called you to his eternal glory in Christ, will himself restore, confirm, strengthen, and establish you."

1 PETER 5:10 (NIV)

Acknowledgments and Gratitude

My Grandmother, Ma: Kathryn Bowers, the woman who raised me, loved me unconditionally, and instilled in me the values of faith, resilience, and love. Ma, your legacy lives on in my heart, and I am eternally grateful for your presence in my life.

My Husband: To my loving husband Brandon, who has been my rock, my partner in parenting, and my unwavering supporter. Your love, understanding, and newly shared journey through life have been my greatest blessings.

My Children: Michael, Josh, Sean, Chloe, Liam, my bonus children Bryce, Brandon Jr., Breanna,and my grandsons Paxton and Kobe you are my greatest treasures. Your love and unwavering support have been my driving force, and I am endlessly proud of the individuals you are becoming.

My Aunt: To my dear aunt, Montrice, who provided refuge and unwavering support during my challenging times. Your home became a sanctuary, and your guidance shaped my journey.

My Dad: To my father, Phillip, who has been a source of love, laughter, and lifelong lessons. Your presence in my life has been a blessing, and I appreciate the memories we've shared.

My Mother: To my mother, Desiree, who taught me about resilience and strength, even in the face of adversity. Your love has always been felt, and I honor the sacrifices you made.

My Step-Mother: To my stepmother, Rena. who played a significant role in my life and contributed to the person I have become. Your presence and support have been appreciated.

My Best Friend: Lakishia, the friend who has been by my side since high school, thank you for your unwavering friendship, support, and shared journey through life's ups and downs.

My Supportive Network: To my crew of friends, colleagues, and mentors who have stood by me, cheered me on, and helped me navigate the challenges of motherhood and a career. Your presence in my life is a gift I cherish.

My Readers: To those who have embarked on this journey with me through the pages of my story, thank you for your time and attention. I hope my story has inspired, encouraged, and touched your hearts in some way.

Resources and References:

For readers who may want to learn more or seek help, I have compiled a list of resources and references that may be valuable:

Parenting and Family Support: Reach out to local community centers, parenting classes, and family support organizations for guidance and assistance in navigating the challenges of parenthood.

Mentorship and Advocacy: Seek out mentorship programs and advocacy groups that offer support and guidance to young mothers and individuals facing adversity.

Mental Health Resources: If you or someone you know is struggling with mental health issues, consider reaching out to a mental health professional or a crisis hotline. There is no shame in seeking help.

Faith and Spiritual Support: Connect with a local faith community or spiritual leader for guidance, support, and a sense of community during challenging times. Thank you to my church, One Accord International.

Educational and Career Resources: Explore educational opportunities, career development programs, and resources available in your community to help you achieve your professional goals.

In closing, I want to extend my heartfelt gratitude to all those who have been a part of my journey. Your love, support, and presence have been invaluable, and I am blessed to have you in my life. As I move forward, I carry with me the lessons, values, and resilience that have defined my story. May we all find the strength to overcome adversity, embrace our faith, and continue to make a positive impact on the world around us.

"Let us not become weary in doing good, for at the proper time we will reap a harvest if we do not give up."

Galatians 6: 9 (NIV)

Made in United States
Orlando, FL
12 January 2024